Terror in Casablanca

A True Story of A Little Girl's Terrifying
Journey Into The Realm of Middle-
Eastern Culture- And her Loss of
Innocence

By

Deborah Gleissner

authorHOUSE™

1663 LIBERTY DRIVE, SUITE 200
BLOOMINGTON, INDIANA 47403
(800) 839-8640
WWW.AUTHORHOUSE.COM

First published by AuthorHouse 10/27/04

ISBN: 1-4208-0157-0 (e)
ISBN: 1-4208-0156-2 (sc)

Printed in the United States of America
Bloomington, Indiana

This book is printed on acid-free paper.

I Would Like to Dedicate This Book To:

My daughter Regina, who made this book a reality.

My daughter Robynne, who made me realize what being a mother was all about.

My husband David, who believes in me and loves me regardless!

My sisters Julie and Cindy who patiently put up with their big sister.

My precious grandson Trae, who gives me bragging rights.

And finally, Larry-Thanks for lending a "helping" hand!

Catherine and Lucy at Authorhouse,

Thank you ladies for you support and guidance.

The Events, Time and Location of
This Story Are True.
The Names Have Been Changed

Table of Contents

I Would Like to Dedicate This Book To:............................v

Prologue:...xiii

Chapter One: England 1953.....................................1

Chapter Two: Southern Indiana 11

Chapter Three: New Mexico..................................17

Chapter Four: Big Move 25

Chapter Five: Casablanca, Morocco......................33

Chapter Six: New Life 41

Chapter Seven: The Bath 47

Chapter Eight: The Apartment..............................59

Chapter Nine: A New Friend.................................65

Chapter Ten: The Abduction 69

Chapter Eleven: Benny...79

Chapter Twelve: The Examination........................85

Chapter Thirteen: Return to the States..................91

Chapter Fourteen: A New Mom 97

Epilogue: 1970...99

But if anyone causes one of these little ones who trusts in me to lose faith, it would be better for that person to be thrown into the sea with a large millstone tied around the neck.

Matthew 18:6

NLT

Prologue:

"Lizzie, stay with mum!" Sarah said with her heavy English accent. Having been in the states for only six years, she already had three children and had traveled extensively across the United States. Now, she was trying to juggle three small children into the local hospital for their overseas immunizations. Sarah's next home would be in Casablanca, Morocco, North Africa. The year was 1959.

now I lay me down to sleep,
I pray the Lord my soul to keep...

Chapter One: England 1953

Sarah's husband Bob had met her when he was stationed in Bushy Park, England. Following a short courtship, they were married near London. Soon after they were married, the Air Force shipped Bob back to the States and Sarah followed shortly after.

"I'll send you the money for your ticket as soon as I can." Bob reassured Sarah as he prepared to leave. Holding her close as the cold winter wind blew across her Kingston home in Surrey, "My tour of duty will be over in just a few months and then we can settle down in a small town where my parents live." Sounding its horn, Bob's taxi pulled into the driveway. Giving Sarah a long kiss good bye, Bob quickly threw his bags into the backseat and waved to Sarah as he pulled away.

Wiping the tears from her face, Sarah ran back to the warm comfort of her country home. Taking refuge in her bedroom, Sarah sat down on her bed and contemplated her future. Gazing down at the new gold band on her left hand, at seventeen she could hardly believe she was married already. She had only known Bob a short six months and here she was getting ready to move to America! She was scared and excited at the same time. What would America be like? What would Bob's family be like? Sarah had read a lot of what the States would be like from her sister who was already there. Her older sister was married and lived in Boston, Massachusetts. The letter sent home told of a life far different than what they had ever experienced. Still, Sarah knew she would miss her family, she was leaving behind. Twisting the gold band on her hand, Sarah smiled at the thought of the children she would have in America. Maybe she was pregnant already? "Oh well," she thought to herself, "Time will tell."

Time seemed to drag by slowly as Sarah waited to hear news from her husband. Checking the mail each day and running to answer the telephone each time it rang. Sarah was anxious to hear from Bob.

The day finally arrived when Sarah and her parents stood waiting at the harbor where the ship sat waiting for her to board. The ship was huge and Sarah swallowed the lump in her throat as she prepared to leave her family and home for a land so far away. She took comfort in knowing that her sister and husband would be there to greet her on her arrival.

Settling in her cabin with another older lady, Sarah's thoughts of home were replaced with the wonder and excitement of her journey to America. Her cabin companion was also going to America for the first time and the two quickly became friends and shared stories of their past and dreams of their futures.

As the ship entered the harbor of New York City, Sarah was amazed at the sights of the city and the Statue of Liberty. She was about to embark on a new adventure and a new life. Standing on the bow of the ship, Sarah anxiously looked for the familiar faces of her sister and husband.

As the ship docked and the passengers eagerly waited to disembark, Sarah tightened the scarf around her neck and took a deep breath. Her knees were shaking. It was February, 1954.

Figure 1: Sarah with Mum about to begin her journey

**Figure 2: Bob standing in uniform, in front of
Mother-in-Law's home**

Figure 3: Sarah with Mum at home

Figure 4: Sarah with her Mum and Dad

Figure 5: Bob at Sarah's home

Figure 6: Sarah leaving home

....daddy's girl....

Chapter Two: Southern Indiana

Settling his new bride in his hometown in southern Indiana, Bob finished his tour of duty and found a local job in a factory. The pay was modest but sufficient.

Anxious to start a life with his young wife, Bob had found a small apartment in his hometown and quickly settled down to small town life. Bob was happy and in love.

Sarah quickly acclimated herself to life in the United States and to Bob's family. Her English accent was a curiosity to everyone and there was no lack of interested listeners as she spoke of her home and family in England.

It wasn't long after arriving in the small southern Indiana town when Sarah soon became pregnant with their first child.

Although Sarah was anxiously awaiting the birth of her first child, pregnancy did not treat her well and she was sick for most of the time. Bob was excited at the prospect of having a son and doted on his wife who was growing larger each week.

The baby was due the 11th of December and Sarah, at 5'2", was alarmingly large for her size. Bob, on the other hand, was extremely egotistical when showing off his wife.

"Anyone can father a child," he would say, "But, it takes a real man to father one like this!"

When Sarah's due date came and went by with no sign of impending labor, she took to her bed and waited impatiently for this "monster of a child" to make his or her appearance. Bob was sure this had to be a boy. No girl could be this big! Christmas also went by and still no baby. Sarah became increasingly alarmed at her past due date and the size of her baby. How would she be able to deliver a child this size?

On the first day of January, 1955, Sarah started her labor. The local newspaper was sponsoring a contest for the first New Year's baby. Bob and Sarah were sure they would win. Sarah's contractions were slow and often stopped for several hours before starting again. A trip to the doctor's office confirmed that her delivery would not be on the first of January. Disappointed, they returned home and waited.

Sarah remained awake the rest of the night as she timed her contractions. The second day of January proved to be the same as the first. Her contractions were sporadic and not close enough to go to the hospital. Sarah, who had now been awake for twenty-four hours was exhausted and wanted desperately to give birth.

"I don't think this child wants to come out!" she complained to her husband.

"Either that, or he hasn't figure out how to get out!" Bob said with a grin.

"Oh please, Bob. I really don't care how she comes out as long as she hurries!" Sarah answered emphasizing the word "she".

On the second night of her on again, off-again contractions, Sarah's water broke and she knew it was time to go to the hospital. The third day of her labor proved to be extremely hard on Sarah and she slept between contractions. This baby was definitely not in any hurry to make its grand appearance. On the fourth day, the doctor told Bob that if they baby did not come within that day; he would perform an emergency caesarean. Sarah could not take much more.

At 5:54 p.m., Sarah gave birth to an 11lb. baby girl. Bob was beside himself with pride. He had forgotten about wanting a son. He had an 11lb girl! And although, theirs was the second baby born that year, his was the biggest and consequently was entitled to a second place win in the paper. Elizabeth had quickly become daddy's girl.

Having just completed three years in the service, Bob became disenchanted with factory work and now with a family to support he decided to re-enlist. The money and benefits looked good.

Figure 7: Sarah with her sister and young nephew

Wish he could turn
back the pages of time....

Chapter Three: New Mexico

Bob spent the next three years stationed at Holloman Air Force Base in New Mexico, during which time; Katie was born on July 4, 1956. Bob had now been promoted and was in charge of training German shepherd attack dogs. Developing a close relationship with one dog, Bob brought him home and introduced him to Elizabeth who was a toddler by now. The dog's new home was under the crawl space of Bob's home and Sarah was constantly running after Lizzie who wanted to go see the doggie. Lizzie was not to be deterred seizing the right opportunity. While her mother and father, were still sleeping in one Saturday morning. Lizzie slipped out the front door. Crouching down to look under the house, Lizzie soon found herself under the belly of a sixty-pound attack dog. Although the dog did her no harm and was merely holding her down, Lizzie's screams brought her father to her rescue in record time. It would be only a few years later, when Bob would look back on this rescue and wish that he could turn back the pages of time.

Then in May of 1958, Bob received orders to go to Morocco. Sarah was once again pregnant with another girl, Caroline.

"Why don't you go live with Mom and Dad until the baby is born and then I'll bring you and the girls to me," advised Bob. Not wanting to give birth in North Africa, Sarah decided to return to Indiana with Bob's parents until the baby was born. Caroline was born on August 5, 1958, two days short of her father's birthday. Upon hearing the news of his daughter's birth, Bob gave up hope on having a son. He was sure that Sarah had, had her share of having babies and would not likely entertain the idea of trying again for number four! Caroline was five months old when her father sent for them to live with him in Morocco.

Sarah was not looking forward to the immunizations, three screaming kids was not her idea of a pleasant day. So, she made a mental not to stop and get some ice cream on the way back home from the doctor's office. Arriving at the doctor's office, Sarah quickly ushered the girls into the waiting room. It was also about this time that Lizzie decided this was not some place she wanted to be. The nurse agreed with Sarah that it might be a good idea to take the two youngest girls first while Sarah waited with Lizzie.

When the nurse returned with Caroline, who was crying and Katie with a tear streaked face, she exchanged kids with Sarah and took Lizzie into the doctor's room. Already in tears, Lizzie looked back at her mother reluctantly.

"Go with the nurse honey, and mummy will get you some ice cream on the way home, Okay?"

A few short minutes later, a blood-curdling scream let Sarah know that Lizzie had received her first shot. Seconds later, Lizzie came streaking out of the doctor's room, tugging at her panties and desperately trying to get out the front door. Lizzie was certain that she did not want the second injection the doctor was preparing when she jumped off the table and bolted out the door. Back in the car, Sarah made a quick stop at the ice cream parlor. The girls seemed to have forgotten the pain of the shots, but Lizzie would remember them a year and a half later.

Sarah was ready for a change of scenery and lifestyle, Bob had wrote her a letter saying that with the currency exchange in Casablanca, they could live like royalty. The thought of that alone made the chore of packing and getting the girls ready for a big move well worth everything.

Figure 8: Lizzie and Bob in Alamagordo, New Mexico

Figure 9: Lizzie 18 months old

...cute kids, he said, looking at Sarah

.

Chapter Four: Big Move

The big day had finally arrived and Bob's dad was taking Sarah and the girls to the airport. With stops and layovers, the trip would take two days and Sarah dreaded the thought of being on an airplane with three kids for that length of time. At the same time she was anxious to see Bob again. He had been gone five months now, and she missed him terribly. Sarah knew that Lizzie missed her daddy too; after all she was daddy's girl.

After boarding the plane, a smiling stewardess came to Sarah's aide.

"You look like you've got your hands full, let me help you strap these two in." she offered

"Yes, they are a handful! Thank you so kindly." Sarah said with a nervous smile.

"You are welcome," replied the stewardess as she fastened the seat belts around Lizzie and Katie. "Would you girls like to color in a coloring book?"

"YES!" Lizzie emphatically as Katie nodded her head shyly.

"Oh, thank you so very much! I'm sure that will keep them occupied." Sarah said in a grateful voice.

Sarah watched as the stewardess strapped the girls in and noticing how pretty the young woman was. Sarah suddenly became self-conscious of her own appearance. Running her fingers through her hair, Sarah thought it had been a lifetime ago since she had a figure to be proud of. She had bore three children in three years and had gained 15 pounds.

Lizzie squirmed as the stewardess strapped her in and the look on her face told Sarah that another fit was about to erupt. Trying to assuage Lizzie's inability to sit still; Sarah calmly pleaded with her young daughter. "Sit still Lizzie and this nice lady will get you a coloring book." That promise seemed to work as Sarah sat back and adjusted Caroline who was sleeping contentedly on her lap. She smiled at her sleeping baby as she thought how different and yet how similar the children were to each other. Caroline seemed to have more of her big sister Lizzie's traits than that of Katie. Katie was quiet and required little attention. She learned quickly following Lizzie's steps, but she wasn't as tempestuous. Caroline, on the other hand was also learning quickly, much too quickly to Sarah's dismay. A loud wail would dictate her emotions if her needs or desires were not met immediately.

Sighing wistfully of days gone by, Sarah turned her attention to her two daughters sitting beside her. It seemed that Lizzie and Katie had turned their attention to the young airman sitting directly across the aisle from them. "Cute kids," He said as he looked at Sarah.

"This one," he said pointing at Lizzie "looks like you."

Suddenly aware of every strand of hair out of place and the milk stains on her navy blue skirt, Sarah's face turned crimson.

"Thank you for the compliment, but I must add that she acts more like her father." Sarah said with a laugh.

"Well, that can't be all bad!" grinning the airman replied

"No, it is not." Sarah said while stroking Lizzie's hair.

"My name is Kenny and I'd be glad to give you a helping hand when you get off."

"Thank you so very much. My name is Sarah and we are on or way to Casablanca where my husband is stationed.

"Great! That's where I'm headed." He replied.

Then as if on cue, the stewardess returned with two color books and two boxes of crayons. Lizzie squealed in anticipation and Katie showed her delight with a broad smile from ear to ear.

"Well that should keep them happy for awhile." Kenny said.

"Yes, I certainly hope so." Sarah replied as the intercom beckoned their attention to the seat belt and no smoking signs. After listening to the carefully enunciated and well-rehearsed message, Sarah sat back and listened as the engines whine rose to a crescendo. The sudden movement of the plane turning onto the runway assured Sarah that she would soon be reunited with her husband.

Figure 10: Passport photograph taken prior to Casablanaca

Figure 11: Lizzie and Katie shortly after moving to Casablanca

....it would only take eighteen months for

him to regret that decision....

Chapter Five: Casablanca, Morocco

Bob was waiting for his family as the plane taxied onto the tarmac. He spotted Sarah as she exited the plane and noticed she was carrying Caroline. Immediately behind Sarah he recognized Katie in the arms of a flight attendant and behind her a young airman was carrying Lizzie.

His heart leaped with the anticipation of seeing his family again, especially Caroline, whom he had not yet seen. Despite his satisfaction of having his family back with him, it would only take eighteen months for him to regret that decision.

Sarah recognized her husband as he weaved his way through a crowd of people who were waiting to greet their own loved ones. "Oh how handsome he is." Sarah thought excitedly as her husband drew near. Aside from his slim build, the first thing you noticed about Bob was his captivating smile and twinkling blue eyes, both of which were inherited by his children.

Lizzie squealed when she recognized her father, prompting Kenny to quickly put her down. Scrambling to her father's arms, Lizzie commanded her father's complete attention by showing him her coloring book that she grasped tightly in her hand. The stewardess deposited Katie gently down beside her father as Kenny gave a wave good-bye.

"Private." Bob called out as Kenny turned to leave, "Thanks, job well done!"

"Sir, Yes Sir." Kenny said with a salute to his superior and then he disappeared into the crowd.

Putting Lizzie back down and then picking up Katie, Bob gave her a hug and kiss as he put his remaining arm around Sarah.

"Baby, I've missed you." He whispered in her ear.

Blushing with her husbands implied statement; Sarah smiled and then waited for him to put Katie down.

"I've missed you too, more than you know." she said as she placed Caroline in his arms.

"Hi Sweetie." crooned Bob as he gazed into Caroline's uncertain eyes. Looking at the unfamiliar face of her father, Caroline then anxiously looked for her mother. Handing Caroline back to her mother, Bob looked down at his two older daughters and kneeling down on one knee and asked, "How have my girls have been? Have you been good for mummy?"

"Yes!" said Lizzie, As they both shook their heads in unison. Then shyly Katie raised her coloring book up to her father and said, "I got a coloring book too!"

"So I see." Bob said as he hugged and kissed each girl tenderly. Standing up and brushing the dust from his uniform pant leg, he continued, "Now let daddy take you girls and mummy to our new house and you can color a picture for daddy, okay?" Looking at his wife and new daughter, Bob took the hands of Lizzie and Katie and asked, "Are you ready?"

"Yes," replied Sarah, "more than ready, I can't wait to see it!"

As they pulled into the driveway of their stucco Mediterranean style home, Bob parked the car in front of the garage. Sarah gasped in surprise.

"I didn't know it would be this nice!"

Grinning like a schoolboy, Bob replied, "Oh it gets better!" Taking her hand Bob led her around to the front of the house as Lizzie and Katie ran excitedly to the rope

Deborah Gleissner

swing that hung from a large tree. Taking a key from his pocket, Bob unlocked the front door and held it open as Sarah entered the front room.

The home had three bedrooms, a fully equipped kitchen and a large living room that had sliding glass doors that led to an enclosed patio. Large ceiling fans cooled the living room and bedrooms. The entire home was enclosed by a concrete wall; giving the children a safe place to play. An iron gate at the driveway provided the only access to the home; giving Bob and Sarah a false sense of security.

Taking Sarah by the hand, Bob led her outside beyond the patio to a small bungalow. "What's this?" Sarah asked. With an impish grin, Bob answered, "Oh, this is the best part!"

"What? Tell me now!" she squealed.

"This is where the kids' nanny and her family will live." Bob said as he put his arm around Sarah.

"Nanny? You got me a nanny?" Sarah asked incredulously.

"Yes." Bob smiled from ear to ear. "I spoke to them yesterday and they will be here tomorrow. They have two children, a boy and a girl and the father will be around in case you need help with anything."

36

"Can we afford that?" Sarah asked.

"Yes sweetie, we can afford that." Bob replied proudly, pointing to the newly acquired stripes on his uniform. "These stripes mean more money and with American money you can have anything your heart desires."

Sarah's head was spinning with excitement as she thought about an impending nanny and her new home. Then suddenly she turned to Bob and asked, "Can they speak English?"

"Good enough to understand what's being said." he said with a laugh.

"Bob this wonderful; I love it!"

"Good! It's all yours."

Looking at Caroline, who was keeping an alert eye on her father, Bob commented, "She looks like Lizzie."

"She acts like Lizzie too!" she said

Taking the baby from Sarah, Bob gently held her and gave her a kiss.

"We'll go tomorrow and buy a bed for her and anything else you might need."

"Great! Speaking of bed, that sounds even better. I'm exhausted." she said with a sigh

Figure 12: Lizzie's first home in Casablanca

Figure 13: Fireplace showing ceramic panther and tapestry

.....the only memory she would carry
back with her from Morocco....

Chapter Six: New Life

Life was drastically different in Morocco than what Sarah had ever experienced before. Getting used to Arabic customs and traditions took Sarah a little longer than what she had hoped for. Fatima, her new nanny, had a limited grasp of English. This did not make things any easier. But for Lizzie and Katie, the language barrier was not a problem. They soon found playmates with Fatima's two children.

Shopping for food was a daily ritual that Sarah enjoyed as she tagged along with Fatima to the outdoor markets. The smell of mint tea reminded Sarah of her home back in England but the strong odor of fresh fish brought her back to reality quite abruptly. The markets were crowded and noisy but exotic. Sarah loved browsing about in the small shops; often bringing home a souvenir that she knew would someday remind her of her stay in Morocco. Unfortunately, these souvenirs would not be the only memory she would take back with her from Morocco.

She decorated her home with a beautiful wall tapestry, a sleek black ceramic panther for her fireplace mantel and odd shaped camel benches that the children loved to straddle. Then there was the silver tea set that she cherished and the leather pocketbook that was better than anything she had ever owned before.

The first year seemed to pass quickly and Sarah noticed that Lizzie and Katie seemed to be picking up the French-Arabic language a little more than what she was comfortable with. More often than not, she would have Bob interpret a new word that Lizzie had learned from her playmates; this usually got Lizzie in trouble.

Getting in trouble was nothing new for Lizzie. She was spirited, strong willed and learned a little too quickly for her own good. More than once, Bob or Sarah would have to come to Lizzie's rescue when she would say something in Arabic to offend a stranger or worse, an offending gesture she had learned! It was times like these that Sarah missed being back in the States again. Caroline was a toddler now and doted after her two big sisters; though she often clashed with Lizzie who had developed an authoritative attitude towards her baby sister.

Although she had now been in Casablanca a year, Sarah was still learning the customs of her adopted country and there were still customs that she was not aware of. It was one of these customs that would change her family's lives forever.

Sarah felt sorry for the limited freedom that Fatima had and the extreme authority that her husband held over Fatima. Sarah and Bob often heard Benny's angry voice directed towards his wife but never heard anything from Fatima. Sarah was so thankful that she had been born and raised in a free world and often wished that Fatima could enjoy the same kind of freedom.

Despite their ethnic differences, Sarah and Fatima had developed a close relationship and were eager to examine social differences. Fatima was amazed and often shocked when Sarah would explain the freedoms she experienced in her marriage and the life she lived in the States.

Figure 17: Katie, Caroline and Lizzie

Figure 18: Caroline and Katie

...he didn't know just how wrong he was...

Chapter Seven: The Bath

Noticing how dirty Fatima's little girl was, Bob suggested to Sarah that maybe she could let the little girl take a bath with their own girls one particular night.

"She smells like she hasn't had a bath in a month." Bob said with disgust.

"Okay, you are probably right." Sarah agreed with a grimace.

Calling out to the girls who were playing in the front yard, Sarah suggested to Lizzie that she bring her little friend in to take a bath with her tonight. Lizzie ecstatically grabbed her playmate by the hand and ran into the house. Never had she been so excited about taking a bath as she was this evening!

As Sarah was letting the girls soak most of the dirt off as they splashed and played, she noticed Fatima looking for her daughter. Stepping out onto the patio, Sarah motioned for Fatima to come into the house. When she took Fatima inside where the girls were playing in the tub, what took place next sent shock waves throughout the entire house!

Fatima screamed in horror as she jerked her daughter out of the bathtub and ran back out of the house with the child crying in fright from her mother's screams. Sarah stood back in shock and confusion over Fatima's reaction to the bath when Bob came running into the bathroom.

"What on earth was that all about?" he asked abruptly.

"I don't know. She acted like I was trying to drown her little girl." Sarah answered cautiously.

"Alright, I'll go out there and see if I can straighten this out." Bob replied reluctantly. Stepping out onto the patio, Bob was met by Benny, who was approaching in a rage.

"Hey Benny, what is wrong?" Bob asked as he put a hand on Benny's shoulder.

Slapping Bob's hand away, Benny spoke in broken English, "You wash my girl in American bath. You disgrace my girl, my family! Now we no longer friends, we must go!" Turning defiantly away he returned to his home.

Fatima was crouched down in the corner of her room holding her daughter and crying, when Benny returned home.

"Why did you let them bathe her?" he yelled as he grabbed his wife and slapped her hard across the face. "She has been disgraced before Allah and our family! No man will want her now!"

As he turned to leave, he left his wife on the floor crying uncontrollably. "We must leave! We cannot stay here! Be ready to go when I return!" he commanded.

Returning to his own home, Bob realized that giving the child a bath was a mistake but he didn't know why. Soothing Sarah and the girls who were visibly upset over what had just happened, Bob assured Sarah that all would be well tomorrow and that Benny and Fatima would get over this. He didn't know just how wrong he was.

The next day, Bob and Sarah discovered that Benny had moved his family out of their small bungalow in the middle of the night and were gone without a goodbye.

"Don't worry. I will get to the bottom of this today!" Bob said as he prepared to go to work.

Asking a fellow airman at work who was aware of Arabic customs, "What did we do wrong?" Bob explained the situation and promptly received an answer to his question.

Ignorant of Arabic customs, Bob and Sarah had committed a serious offense by bathing the little girl in their bathtub. Benny's religion allowed bathing only on certain days and only in certain rivers. A comrade at work warned Bob to be careful, "These people believe in eye for an eye if you wrong them." Returning home that evening, Bob felt terrible about his mistake and wanted to apologize to Benny, but was unable to find him.

Two days later, Benny had apparently returned during the night but it was not to say goodbye. Bob had discovered a chilling not wrote in Arabic pinned to his door with a six inch dagger!

Bob swallowed hard as his blood ran cold. *What does this mean?* "Keep the girls in the house today! I am going to find out what this means." Bob instructed Sarah as he prepared to go to work.

Showing the note to his commanding officer, Bob asked to find someone who could read the note.

"Yeah, Rashid over there could tell you what it means. What on earth did you do to deserve this?" asked his commanding officer in a puzzled tone. Explaining the story, Bob quickly approached Rashid and asked him to interpret the note. Handing the note quickly back to Bob, Rashid's dark features took on an ashen quality. "You, my friend are in grave danger!" he said desperately. "You must move your family immediately! This is a death threat to your family!"

Relaying this information to his commanding officer, Bob was able to return home early that day. As he bolted through the front door, a surprised Sarah asked, "What are you doing home so early?"

"You have got to start packing. We have to move."

Frightened by the tone of alarm in Bob's voice, Sarah asked, "But Why? What did the note say?"

"It was a death threat to all of us and we have to get out of here. There is an apartment in town that we can move into," he continued, "I'm going to town while you start packing."

"Bob, I'm scared! I want to go back home." Sarah said choking back tears.

"I know sweetheart, but that will take time and right now we don't have much of that." He said holding Sarah in his arms. "We can get an apartment right now and I'll put in for a transfer as soon as I can."

"Okay, I'll start packing now." Sarah said seeking refuge in her husband's arms.

As Bob started out the front door, he once again cautioned Sarah to keep the girls inside. He had lost the twinkle in his eyes and his easy smile was replaced with a clenched jaw. Sarah was tired of packing and unpacking and found herself dreaming of the day when she could stay in one place longer than a year. She thought of her home and Mum back in England and a time when life didn't seem so complicated, of her sister who lived in Boston, Massachusetts and how lucky she was to live in the same house for several years, to actually have roots. All she wanted to do now was get out of North Africa.

Lizzie, not understanding the situation, gave Sarah a difficult time with her incessant whining and crying.

"I want to SWING!" Lizzie cried defiantly.

"No, love, you can't go out now. Daddy wants you girls to stay inside for awhile. Why don't you and Katie go play with you dollies and mummy will give you a cookie, okay?"

That seemed to appease Lizzie for the time being. Sarah went to the garage to retrieve some boxes. As she stepped out the door and turned on the light, her blood ran cold. Crawling all over the concrete floor were several poisonous scorpions. Slamming the door behind her as she ran back inside, Sarah bolted the door to keep Lizzie from getting into the garage. "How did they get in there?" She had seen only one since moving here and that was outside of the concrete walls that guarded their home. "Why didn't Bob see them when he left earlier?" A chill ran up her spine. "Someone must have put them there after Bob left." She ran through the house making sure all the windows and doors were locked. After checking on the girls playing in their bedroom, Sarah went to her own room and broke down in tears. She was scared and homesick. *Was this all because she gave that little girl a bath?* Drying her tears, Sarah got busy gathering things to pack into boxes for when Bob returned home.

A short time later, she heard Bob pull into the garage and then he abruptly, backed out again. Sarah ran to the front door and unlocked it. Seeing the look of terror on Sarah's face, Bob realized that Sarah was already aware of the scorpions.

"Get me a large jar, I'm going to put them in gasoline." He said clenching his jaw in anger. Hearing her father's return, Lizzie ran out of the bedroom and fastened herself to her father's leg. "I want to swing." She cried.

"Not now, honey you could get hurt outside. Daddy will show you why in just a minute," he replied as he retrieved a pair of tongs from the kitchen drawer. Sarah held both the girls back as Bob cautiously entered the garage. Keeping one eye on the scorpions, he quickly poured gasoline into the glass jar. Surveying his surrounding to make sure there were none hanging over his head, he quickly picked each one up and submerged them with the gasoline. Bob counted to ten, knowing this was only the beginning.

Bringing the jar into the house, he set it down on the kitchen counter. The girls quickly gathered around to inspect their father's find. Bob took a deep breath and looked at Sarah as they knew each others thoughts. Looking down at Lizzie and Katie, in a serious tone he said, "See their tails, they can sting you badly and make you very sick. That's why you can't go outside and play."

"Can they sting me now?" Lizzie asked curiously staring at the odd creatures.

"No, sweetheart, the gasoline killed them. But, this is why you must stay inside until mummy or daddy say that you may go outside. Okay?" he said sternly.

Lizzie and Katie, noting the serious tone of their fathers warning shook their heads silently in solemn understanding. Taking control of the girls silence Sarah told them to return to their room.

"Can you get those boxes for me?" she asked turning towards Bob.

Massaging the stiffness from his neck he replied, "Yeah, and now that this is over we have an apartment to move into tomorrow."

"Good!" she said showing a little enthusiasm. Although she already knew the answer she asked, "Bob, how do you think they got into the garage?"

"There is no doubt in my mind that someone deliberately put them there." He said quietly.

"You don't think Benny put them there, do you?"

"I don't know for sure, but it sure looks that way!" he snapped.

After putting the girls to bed, Sarah worked feverishly into the night packing. She was looking forward to getting out of the house. Yet, it was only a year ago that she had moved in, excited beyond measure. That was all gone now. Despite her disappointment, she was happy to discover boxes that had yet to be unpacked. It was one less thing for her to take care of.

Figure 14: Family Picture showing Benny holding Caroline

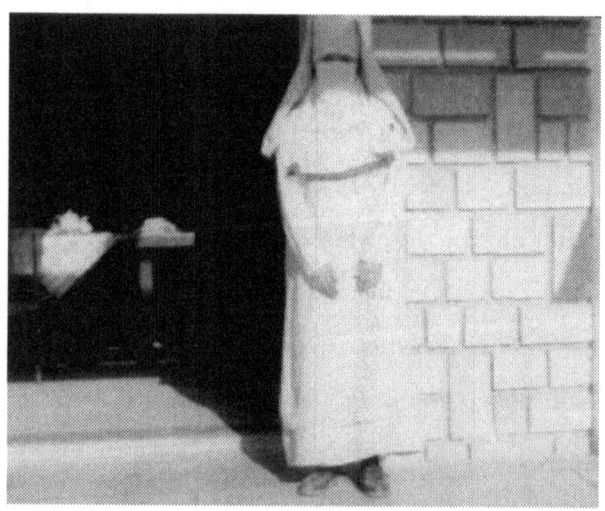

Figure 15: Benny's wife Fatima

...there was someone out there who wanted to hurt his family....

Chapter Eight: The Apartment

The morning sunshine came much too early for Sarah who found little sleep the previous night; but the anticipation of moving gave her renewed strength.

The events of the previous week had made its mark on Bob, as well. The twinkle in his eye was gone, his smile replaced with a clenched jaw.

"*No one,*" he thought "*will get away with threatening my family.*"

Hiring a rickety truck to move their belongings was an easy feat and by the end of the day the family was once again exploring new territory. The apartment was small with only two bedrooms, a far cry from the spacious home they had left behind. Lizzie however was fascinated with the two story balcony that overlooked the playground below.

"How about I take the girls to the playground while you unpack a few things?" Bob suggested.

"Great!" Sarah smiled, standing amidst a pile of boxes wondering where to begin. "While you are out, maybe you could find something for dinner?"

"Come on girls; let's see what we can find." Bob said as he ushered the two girls out the door.

Picking Katie up on his hip, Bob held a tight grip on Lizzie's hand as he made his way down a narrow staircase to the outer courtyard. The apartment complex was made up of three large buildings that surrounded an inner courtyard. There was a playground on one end of the courtyard and an open air market at the other end. The smell of freshly cooked meats caught Bob's attention. He decided to give the girls another fifteen minutes as he looked at his watch. He knew that trying to drag them away now was not something he wanted to even negotiate. He pulled out a cigarette and lit it while surveying his surroundings. The atmosphere of the courtyard was peaceful and relaxed, he watched women wander in and out of the various fruit and vegetable stands. Children were running about with no apparent supervision. But somewhere out there, there was someone who wanted to hurt his family.

He knew he had to get his family back to the States on safe ground, but at the same time, he realized the process of getting a transfer was something that would take time. He had already submitted the transfer now all he could do was watch and wait. It was the watching part that made his blood run cold.

"Daddy, push me higher!" Lizzie squealed interrupting his thoughts. "Me too!" added Katie not to be outdone by her older sister.

"Okay, one more push and then we have to go find something for dinner. Daddy's hungry!"

"Me too!" the girls' voices echoed.

"Oh good, you have dinner!" Sarah exclaimed as Bob and the girls came through the front door. Placing the food on their makeshift table, Bob held back a grin anticipating Sarah's reaction to what he bought for dinner.

"What is on those sticks?" Sarah asked cautiously placing the dishes on the table.

"Rattlesnake," Bob replied with his familiar impish grin.

"Rattlesnake?" Sarah asked incredulously, "You brought bloody rattlesnake?"

"No, it's not bloody, it is cooked." Bob replied still grinning. "Try it; I think you might like it."

"Rattlesnake!" Sarah said shaking her head with indignation, putting small pieces on the girl's plates. "Wait until mum hears about this!"

"Yeah, my ears are burning already." Bob said as he helped himself to another piece.

Figure 16: A view of Downtown Casablanca

...this persistence....wore down Sarah's

resolve...........

Chapter Nine: A New Friend

After a few weeks, Sarah and the girls settled into apartment life and Sarah put the past events behind her. It was not long after, that Sarah met another American family living in the adjoining building. Making friends with someone else who spoke English was a God Send. Her new friend Laura, made each day in the desert a little more bearable. They shared stories of home and family.

Chaperoning the girls as they played outside became an event Sarah looked forward to; having another adult to talk to. None the less, the constant chaperoning became time consuming with Lizzie's constant whining to go outside. It was this persistence that wore down Sarah's resolve not to let her daughter go out by herself.

"Lizzie, if mummy lets you go out and play, you must stay where mummy can see you from the balcony, okay" Sarah offered after a particularly hard morning with Lizzie.

"Okay, mummy, can I go out now?" pleaded Lizzie.

"Yes, and take your sand bucket with you to use in the sandbox."

Putting Katie and Caroline down for their naps, Sarah then pulled a chair to the balcony where she could keep an eye on Lizzie. Watching her daughter play with the other children, Sarah became lost in her own thoughts. Lizzie had grown so fast and seemed smarter than the other children her age and maybe, she thought, a little too smart for her own good!

Indeed, Lizzie was smart beyond her age and she knew how to manipulate her mother when it came to getting her way. Lizzie's strong-willed temperament was construed as her "spirit" according to her fathers' interpretation. It was her fathers' intention that Lizzie's "spirit" not be broken, and therefore, Lizzie had daddy wrapped around her finger.

A month had passed now with no more threats and Sarah's vigilance over Lizzie was beginning to wane. It was this lack of concern that would lead to the most traumatic experience that Lizzie would ever go through.

......offering the coveted piece

of candy.....

Chapter Ten: The Abduction

There was no apparent speed limit, no obvious right of way and no reason to give consideration to courtesy when it came to traffic in downtown Casablanca. Sarah was to find this out when she decided to venture out on her own one day on a shopping spree. She left the children with their new found friend, Laura to baby sit. Sarah took the taxi to town. It was the return trip home that nearly ended in disaster when Sarah's taxi and another collided. The impact sent Sarah and her packages sprawling all over the back seat, resulting in a wrenched back for Sarah. Sarah had been warned previously about the local hospitals and decided she would be better off nursing herself at home.

The next few days found Sarah resting on the sofa if she was not watching Lizzie on the playground.

Caroline was a toddler now and a constant irritation to Katie who was content to sit at the table and color. Caroline's approach to play consisted of grabbing Katie's crayons and breaking them in half or simply eating them. Caroline's smile often boasted of brightly colored teeth much to Sarah's dismay. It was one of these kinds of squabbles that led Sarah from her perch on the balcony and out of Lizzie's sight.

Lizzie was showing her playmate how to build a sand castle using her bucket packed with sand. It was then, that she noticed a crowd of children gathering around a candy stand. Someone was giving away candy! Looking up to the balcony, Lizzie could see that her mother was gone. That gave Lizzie the opportunity she needed to get in line with the other children. As the line grew smaller and Lizzie came closer to the stranger giving out candy, she suddenly recognized the man. It was Benny!

Coming to Katie's rescue, Sarah retrieved crayons from Caroline's grasp and immediately inspected her mouth. Just as she expected Caroline had green teeth and Sarah spent the next few minutes cleaning Caroline's teeth. In an effort to pacify Caroline's need to eat anything in her grasp, Sarah went to the kitchen cabinet and brought out a bag of cookies. After giving each of the girls a cookie, Sarah, still nursing a sore back, slowly made her way halfway to the balcony when a knock on the door interrupted her progress.

Benny smiled at Lizzie as she reached toward his hand offering the coveted piece of candy. Suddenly, grabbing her hand, Benny's smile was gone and his dark eyes reflected a murderous gleam. Lizzie, shocked at Benny suddenly grabbing her hand was confounded even more with the disappointment of not getting the piece of candy he had offered. Struggling to pull her hand away, her fear escalated when Benny proceeded to drag her away from the crowd.

Answering the door, Sarah was glad to see her friend had come for a visit. Before returning to her guest, Sarah returned to the balcony to get a quick check on Lizzie. Thinking that she could see Lizzie in the crowd of children, Sarah returned to her guest settling down to coffee and cigarettes.

As Benny pulled Lizzie through the courtyard, paralyzing fear turned Lizzie's cries into whimpers. Looking over her shoulder, Lizzie desperately wanted to see her mother on the balcony, but she was not there. Digging her heels into the dirt, Lizzie tried desperately to pull away from her captor's grip. Her efforts were useless and the growing lump in her throat prevented her from crying out for help. Where was he taking her? Where was her mummy? Benny was taking Lizzie to the adjoining building and her hopes were lifted. Mummy's friend lives her! As they entered the building, Benny mysteriously started knocking on all the doors. He would knock two times, hardly giving anyone time to answer and then he would quickly leave. After going up to the second floor, Benny started knocking on the doors again.

What was he doing? Lizzie thought as her mind raced. Her fears had tempered when she realized they were approaching the apartment where her mummy's friend lived. She knew mummy's friend would help her. Her apartment was the last one at the end of the hall and Lizzie could see the door. Lizzie kept her exuberance at bay when Benny stopped and knocked at the door. But once again, he only knocked twice and then quickly left. *Please come to the door!* Lizzie cried to herself. The lump that had disappeared when Lizzie realized that her rescue was at hand suddenly reappeared when Benny started up the third flight of stairs.

Sarah, deciding it was time for Lizzie to come back in went to the balcony to call for her daughter. Looking over the crowd of children, Sarah could not see Lizzie.

Asking her friend to watch over Katie and Caroline, Sarah went down to the playground to look for Lizzie, but Lizzie was no where to be found. Searching the playground, Sarah found Lizzie's sand bucket but her daughter was gone. Fear overtook Sarah as the events of only a few months ago quickly came back to her memory. Racing frantically over the playground and around the courtyard, Sarah repeatedly called out for Lizzie. Remembering Bob's warnings to watch the girls and to not let Lizzie go out by herself, Sarah began to cry, "Where are you Lizzie?" Deciding to return to her apartment in hopes that maybe Lizzie had returned home on her own, Sarah had forgotten about the pain in her back. She was overcome with fear for her five year old daughter.

As they reached the top floor, Lizzie recognized the door that led to the roof. This is where mummy hangs her clothes to dry. Pulling Lizzie through the door, Benny stopped and nervously looked around. There were several clothes lines installed there but no one else was around. Grabbing Lizzie by both shoulders, Benny positioned Lizzie to face him as he knelt to his knees. Spitting in her face, he spoke words in Arabic that she could not understand. Lizzie started crying loudly this time and suddenly Benny pulled on both of her overall straps, dropping them to her feet. Pushing her to the floor, Benny then pulled down his own pants and then Lizzie's panties. Lizzie couldn't understand what was happening and upon seeing Benny pull down his own pants and then hers, Lizzie let out a scream. Slapping his hand over Lizzie's face, Benny attempted to rape her vaginally. When Lizzie's screams became more than what Benny could silence, he then began to strangle her. This caused Lizzie to lose consciousness momentarily. Realizing that his attempts to rape her vaginally were in vain due to her small size, Benny turned Lizzie over and sodomized her. Lizzie regained consciousness and once again started screaming. Benny was hurting her and she did not know how or why. Then suddenly, Benny jumped to her feet, run out the door and was gone. Had someone heard her screams? Was someone coming? Lizzie, despite the tremendous pain, picked herself up from the floor and pulled up her panties and overalls. Cautiously approaching the door, Lizzie looked around for Benny. Seeing that he was nowhere to be seen, Lizzie quickly made her way back down three flights of stairs. She was on her way back home to mummy.

Sarah, running back to her apartment, burst into the front room. Surprised at Sarah's abrupt entrance, Laura asked what was wrong.

"I can't find Lizzie, She's gone!" cried Sarah

"Do you want me to call the police?" Laura asked

"Yes," replied Sarah, "but first I must call Bob."

In a matter of fact tone, Laura said "give me the number and I will call for you."

Giving her friend the necessary numbers, Sarah then returned to the balcony hoping to get a glimpse of her little girl. Clinging to the railing, Sarah broke down in uncontrollable sobs. "Lizzie, where are you?" she cried, "This is all, my fault!"

Coming out to the balcony in an effort to comfort Sarah, Laura put her arms around Sarah's shoulders. "Come sit down on the sofa," she said, "Bob and the police are one their way."

Figure 19: Lizzie on swing beside blue bicycle

......Sarah run to the kitchen

sink and threw up....

Chapter Eleven: Benny

Clutching the straps of her overalls, Lizzie quickly crossed the courtyard and was approaching her own apartment when she spotted Benny on his blue bicycle, hiding behind a fruit stand. Lizzie waited until Benny was out of sight and then ran frantically to her apartment. Bursting through the door, Lizzie caught her mother and neighbor by surprise.

Jumping to her feet, Sarah embraced Lizzie with immeasurable relief but at the same time, she knew something was terribly wrong. Lizzie's dirty face was tear-streaked and she was clutching her overall straps. Looking her daughter over, Sarah noticed that Lizzie had an angry red welt across the left side of her face and the beginning of a black eye. Red finger like bruises around

Lizzie's neck sent Sarah into a further state of shock. Holding back her tears, Sarah asked,

"Lizzie, sweetie, what's wrong where have you been?"

Letting her fear and pain come forth in a torrent of emotion, Lizzie cried out, "He hurt me!"

"Who hurt you, honey?" Sarah asked as mounting fear welled up inside her.

"He pulled my panties down and laid on top of me and hurt me!" Lizzie cried out again.

"Oh, My God!" Laura cried out as she rushed to Sarah and Lizzie's side.

The room started swimming as Sarah, clinging to her daughter realized what Lizzie was trying to say. In an attempt to verify Lizzie's claim, Sarah asked, "Where did he hurt you?"

In a renewed fit of tears, Lizzie let go of her overalls and pointed to her panties still wedged between her thighs. The evidence of her sodomy was evident when Sarah noticed that Lizzie had defecated in her overalls.

"Dear Mary, Sweet mother of God!" exclaimed Sarah as she sank to the floor beside Lizzie.

"Sarah, come sit down here." offered Laura, "and I'll take Lizzie to the bathroom." Sarah's friend was beside herself in shock and horror at what had happened to Lizzie, but she knew she had to be in control now for Sarah's sake.

As Laura was in the bathroom with Lizzie, Sarah ran to the kitchen sink and threw up. The other children stood by quietly, confused by what was taking place. When Sarah ran to the kitchen sink, Katie started crying. Knowing that she had to get control of herself, Sarah comforted Katie, "Mummy is okay now, but I have to help Lizzie." With that said, Sarah proceeded to the bathroom where Laura was gently cleaning up Lizzie. "

"Can you get me some clean clothes?" Laura asked as Sarah entered the bathroom.

"Yes." Sarah said quickly, returning to the girls' bedroom. As she was rummaging through Lizzie's clothing, the sound of approaching sirens filled the room. Only seconds later, Bob charged through the front door along with two policemen. With Lizzie and Laura still in the bathroom, Sarah rushed to meet her husband.

"What's happened? Where's Lizzie?" Bob asked in alarm.

"Oh, Bob, she's here but she's hurt!" cried Sarah, "It's all, my fault!"

Hearing her father's voice, Lizzie came running from the bathroom.

"Daddy!" cried Lizzie as she ran to her father's arms, "He hurt me!"

"Who hurt you, Lizzie?"

"That Man" Lizzie answered as she buried her head into her father's shoulder.

With fear and confusion, Bob carefully examined Lizzie's face and neck. Bob looked to Sarah for an answer. Sarah sitting on the sofa, was holding her head in her hands crying uncontrollably. Then looking at Laura, Bob, unable to control his emotions, yelled,

"What in the hell is going on here? How is Lizzie hurt?"

Swallowing the lump in her throat, Laura quietly answered Bob's questions. "Bob, you need to take Lizzie to the hospital, we think she's been raped."

......she simply answered, "Benny"....

Chapter Twelve: The Examination

Bob's face froze momentarily as the realization of Lizzie's rape sank in. Then suddenly, hugging Lizzie as if to protect her from further harm; Bob uttered under his breath, "I'll kill him!"

Looking back at Laura, Bob asked her if she could watch the other children while they were gone. Then Bob looked at Sarah and simply said, "Come on, let's go."

After arriving at the hospital, Sarah stayed with Lizzie while Bob and the two policemen made a report. The doctor performing the examination on Lizzie, took notice of the marks on her face and neck and the evidence of the sodomy was unmistakable. But when the doctor asked Lizzie if the man laid on her tummy, Lizzie remembered the vaccination shots she had received and feared she would receive more is she said yes, so she said "No."

Further examination proved her denial to be false, and the doctor agreed with Sarah that her denial of vaginal rape was simply due to fear and trauma. The rectal tears were minimal prompting the doctor to release Lizzie with a prescription for antibiotics and ointments. He assured Sarah that Lizzie would recover from her physical injuries. Yet, also cautioned her over possible emotional problems that Lizzie might encounter due to her experience. Post-traumatic stress syndrome was not uncommon for children who had suffered through an event such as this and for Lizzie, it was almost a certainty. The doctor gave Bob and the policemen a detailed report of his medical evaluation on Lizzie and released her to go home.

The two policemen escorted Bob and his family home. Despite the relative safety of being home, Lizzie clung to her father. When Bob asked her what the man looked like, she simply answered, "Benny." Recalling the moment she saw Benny on his bicycle, she continued, " I saw him on his bicycle." The policeman kneeling down beside Lizzie asked her, " What color was his bicycle?"

With the memories of her ordeal only a few hours old, mounting fear caused a familiar lump in her throat and she whispered, "Blue." Not wanting to cause her anymore distress, the officer stroked her hair and replied, "That's okay sweetie, he will not hurt you anymore."

A phone call to his commanding officer, relieved Bob from duty the remainder of the day and the policemen left to begin their search for Benny. Bob had never felt such and over-whelming sense of anger in his entire life. Unfortunately, a large part of his anger was directed towards Sarah who had failed to watch Lizzie as he had warned her to do. Not wanting to upset Lizzie any further, Bob kept his anger at bay for the moment as he asked Sarah for a detailed account of the day's activities. When she explained to him how Lizzie was insistent on going out to play and she agreed as long as she could watch Lizzie from the balcony, Bob became a little more understanding of the circumstances. He was well aware of Lizzie's temper tantrums, as a way of getting her way. He was also aware of the physical discomfort that Sarah was going through with her back injury. However, he couldn't dismiss the fact that due to Sarah's lack of supervision, his little girl had been raped and nearly killed.

At work the next day, Bob explained the situation to his commander and asked for an expedition on his request to transfer back to the states. His request was granted and within a week, Bob and his family were on their way back home.

.....was he doing the right thing?

Chapter Thirteen: Return to the States

The move back to the states was quick and uneventful. Lizzie had become subdued and displayed separation anxiety when her father was not in her sight. Bob and Sarah now found Lizzie crawling into their bed at night.

"I'm worried about Lizzie." Sarah commented to Bob one evening. "I can't get her to sleep in her own bed anymore."

"It will take time for her to get over this, hopefully she'll forget soon." Bob replied.

Bob finished his tour of duty in Plattsburgh, New York and relocated his family to Biloxi, Mississippi. There he and Sarah both found local jobs and Lizzie started first grade.

Sarah hired a young black girl to baby-sit the children while she worked. Problems with Lizzie arose when she and her sisters were forced to go to the baby-sitters home. Lizzie related the baby-sitter's father to Benny due to his dark color. Lizzie pushed both her sisters into a corner and stood in front of them in an apparent attempt to protect them for that man. The next day, the baby-sitter was allowed to watch the children at their own home.

Sarah's guilt and Bob's anger escalated resulting in frequent arguments. Lizzie's temperament had also changed and she was less tolerant of Sarah's instruction. Lizzie's first grade teacher also complained about Lizzie's inability to listen and an insatiable need for attention. She also reported that Lizzie showed an unusual display of aggression towards her black playmates. The events of the past year compiled with too many moves took its toll on Bob and Sarah's marriage and they divorce a year after moving to Mississippi.

Bob left Mississippi to live with his parents in Indiana and took Lizzie with him. The decision to relinquish custody of Lizzie to Bob was a difficult one for Sarah but Lizzie's insistence on staying with her daddy was not something Sarah could ignore.

The bus trip in Indiana was a difficult trip for Bob and Lizzie. Lizzie cried for most of the trip when she realized she would not be seeing her mother or sisters for a long time. Bob worried over taking Lizzie from her mother and sisters. Was he doing the right thing? Arriving in Indiana, Bob was met at the bus station by his father. Unaware of past events, Bob's father sat quietly as Bob recounted the story of Lizzie's rape and the resulting problems he encountered with Sarah. Lizzie's grandfather said nothing as his eyes filled with tears. Lizzie was sleeping in the backseat and heard nothing of the ensuing conversation between her father and grandfather.

Settling down in the same town where Lizzie had been born six years prior, Bob soon acquired a job in the same factory he had been working in when Lizzie was born. Lizzie's separation anxiety became more apparent when Bob started working and she was left in the care of her grandmother. Bob quickly enrolled Lizzie in school hoping to establish a normal routine for her again. Despite his efforts Bob realized that he needed help in raising Lizzie. He often found her crying in a secluded place and her depression was due to the absence of her sisters. But the nightmares that brought

Lizzie to her father's bed at night was what gave Bob his biggest concern over Lizzie's mental well-being. He set out to find a mother for Lizzie with hopes of later getting custody of his two younger daughters. Little did he know that finding a new mother would only add to Lizzie's despair.

Figure 3: Lizzie's First Grade Picture

.....in hopes that she
would forget.....

Chapter Fourteen: A New Mom

It had been a short six months when Bob introduced Lizzie to the woman who would soon be her new mother. The transition was fairly smooth during Lizzie's first year, however, there was trouble brewing on the horizon. It seemed Bob's new wife had grown jealous of Bob's devotion to his daughter and Lizzie's demand for her father's attention. Lizzie's nightmares continued along with her nightly visits to her father's bed. Bob was at a loss for a closure to Lizzie's problems. It seemed that his new wife was unable to comfort Lizzie when she needed it the most and more often than not, opted to engage in battles of will.

Lizzie had retained her knowledge of the French-Arabic language and often cursed at her new mother knowing that she would not know what was being said.   An occasional finger often accompanied these outbursts as Lizzie ran out the front door. But Bob's real concern was what Lizzie remembered concerning her abduction. He knew Lizzie needed professional help, but he also knew that he could not afford the cost of a child psychologist. He refrained from speaking to Lizzie about her ordeal in hopes that she would forget. What Bob did not realize, was that Lizzie did remember much more than what he feared.

Epilogue: 1970

Lizzie was 15 years old now and still yearned for answers to questions that haunted her concerning the abduction and rape that remained so vivid in her mind. Her father never mentioned the incident to her and it seemed to Lizzie that the subject was not one to be discussed.

Building up her courage to approach the subject, Lizzie confronted her father. "Dad, you remember what happened in Morocco?" Taken aback by Lizzie's sudden question, Bob's eyes took on an icy glare. "Yes" he replied reluctantly.

"Well" Lizzie continued cautiously, "I was kind of wondering what ever happened to him."

Without saying a word, Bob looked at Lizzie and drew his index finger across his own neck. With a look of shock and disbelief at this revelation, Lizzie turned and walked away not wanting to push the matter any further. It was over.. Or was it?

About the Book

Lizzie was a strong willed precocious five year old and she was "Daddy's Girl." This true story takes Lizzy and her family to Casablanca, Morocco, where her father was stationed in the United States Air Force. Learning the language and customs of the French-Arabic people was difficult at best. For Lizzie's mother Sarah, it was this lack of knowledge that nearly ended her young daughter's life. The story starts in England where Lizzie's mother and father were married, and ultimately peaks in Casablanca, Morocco. This is the story of the consequence of ignorance and the radicalism of religion.